YEMEN: PREVENTING THE NEXT AFGHANISTAN

The sounds of gunfire from tanks and artillery signaled the return of Yemeni President Ali Abdullah Saleh to Yemen on 23 September 2011. Pro-democracy protesters, emboldened by the presence of members of the First Armored Division who had recently defected to the anti-government cause, stood fast in their encampment in "Change" square in downtown Sana'a. Forces loyal to the government, commanded by a son of President Saleh, launched a savage dawn attack on the opposition forces, killing 40 in the first day of fighting.[1] Snipers fired on protesters from rooftops killing and wounding scores. In the following days, artillery shells slammed into parts of the city and government security forces fired on protesters from rooftops claiming another 100 lives.[2] For the past forty years, factions have racked Yemen with rebellion, instability and oppression. The pro-democracy protestors believed their non-violent demonstration would bring about peaceful change, but the Saleh government responded with the Yemeni status quo – violence. Despite the bloodshed, the opposition held its ground and, months later, brought sweeping change in Yemen.

On 23 November 2011 after ten months of protests, government crackdowns and opposition counterattacks, Yemeni President Ali Abdullah Saleh signed the Gulf Cooperation Council's transition of power agreement. This landmark accord called for President Saleh to step down, Yemeni government and opposition factions to form a national unity government and to hold presidential elections within 90 days. President Barak Obama praised Saleh's actions and proclaimed that this action brings the Yemeni people significantly closer to "realizing their aspirations for a new beginning in Yemen."[3]

Despite the US President's optimism, Yemen's new beginning will likely be stillborn. The country is mired in thick political discord, is suffering from an anemic economy, and is rapidly depleting already scarce natural resources. Further, Yemen has deep ethnic and religious divisions, faces a lethal and determined insurgent movement, and plays host to a variety of radical Islamic terrorists. Prior to Saleh's agreement to step down, a confusing and conflicted US-Yemeni policy complicated the situation and demonstrated that the US' strategy required immediate change. Already a "fragile" or "failing" state, continued unrest, instability and uncertainty will undoubtedly push Yemen towards full-fledged failure. Alone, Yemen is unlikely to arrest these negative trends but could benefit from substantial regional and international support. Because of US vital interests in Yemen and the greater Arabian Peninsula, the US has an opportunity to demonstrate international leadership, assist the Yemeni people and protect US interests by developing and implementing a new sound, comprehensive US – Yemeni policy.

While it is infeasible to chronicle all of Yemen's extensive history of political and economic instability, the intricacy of the current political situation and the uncertainty of the nation's future makes possible this critical overview to assist national security decision makers. Beginning with a summary of Yemen's current domestic situation and geopolitical significance, this paper draws attention to the gravity and immediacy of Yemen's extensive problems. Then it examines past and current US-Yemeni policy, US regional and national interests and identifies other regional actors and influences that will affect any future actions to arrest Yemen's rapidly deteriorating security and economic situation. Next, the paper describes several opportunities and associated recommendations that the US should act upon to help stabilize Yemen and concludes by highlighting several of the risks associated with action and inaction.

The Catalyst for Change – Why Yemen? And Why Now?

The Yemen of yesterday will not be the Yemen of the future. If the signposts of the past are any guide, lack of opportunity, persistent conflict, suffering and terror will characterize Yemen's future. However, this future is not preordained. Because of recent events, the US has a once-in-a-generation foreign policy opportunity to shape the future of this potentially dangerous and strategic nation. So, why Yemen? And why now?

Yemen is not a commonly mentioned country in the US. Nor has Yemen ever been a noteworthy object of US foreign policy, popular culture or sustained significant global interest. Of course, before 2001 neither was Afghanistan. This is all changing now. In 2009, Senator Joseph Lieberman stated, "Iraq was yesterday's war, Afghanistan is today's war. If we don't act preemptively, Yemen will be tomorrow's war."[4]

Further, according to former US Ambassador to Yemen, Edmund Hull, Yemen currently has all the negative attributes necessary to maintain, sustain and even increase the power of international terrorists. It has isolated tracts of land, a weak government that cannot project power to the "peripheries," the presence of Islamic jihadists that form a base of support for terrorism, a local population that tolerates or supports the jihadists and a large "distribution of weapons among the people."[5] While numbers and estimates vary, Yemen is clearly the most heavily armed country in the Middle East with at least 32 percent and perhaps as much as 90 percent of its citizens possessing a weapon.[6] With instability and ready access to weapons, it is not surprising that Yemen has become an irresistible terrorist magnet.

Yemen is currently home to Al Qaeda in the Arabian Peninsula (AQAP), the second most significant concentration of Al Qaeda in the Middle East. Since 2010, the Central Intelligence Agency has labeled AQAP as the most dangerous threat to the US homeland, surpassing "that from al-Qaeda in Afghanistan or Pakistan."[7] In 2009, terrorist elements from Saudi Arabia and Yemen pledged allegiance to Al Qaeda and formed the AQAP "regional franchise."[8] Since its founding, AQAP has taken the lead on offensive terror operations against the US mainland and against US regional allies. AQAP claimed responsibility for Umar Farouk Abdulmutallab's 2009 Christmas "underwear" bombing attempt over Detroit, for the 2010 Midwest "toner cartridge" bombs and for inspiring Major Nidal Hasan's 2009 Fort Hood shooting spree.[9] Despite the successful September 2009 drone strike that killed AQAP's leader Anwar al-Awlaki, the organization remains "an innovative, fast-learning, and opportunistic group," whose master bomb maker Ibrahim Hassan Asiri, among other terror leaders, continues to constitute a clear threat to the US mainland and stability in Yemen and the Middle East.[10]

Defeating Al Qaeda abroad, in the near-term, requires the US to operate in Yemen, and therefore requires close cooperation with an undetermined future Yemeni government. Denying the terrorist sanctuary, discrediting the terrorist message and permanently dismantling its operations require a long-term change of conditions in Yemen and decisive action by a proactive Yemeni government and populace.

Yemen, despite its small size and relative obscurity, sits in a strategic location that is increasingly vital to global commerce and energy security, as well as stability. Yemen sits on the southern end of the Arabian Peninsula separated from the volatile

Horn of Africa by a few miles of a key ocean shipping passage. One of the region's oil producing nations, Yemen possesses estimated oil reserves of 3 billion barrels of light sweet crude and 17 trillion cubic feet of natural gas.[11] While not a significant producer of oil compared to other Middle Eastern nations, Yemen's geographic position is critical to the flow of oil from larger Middle Eastern producers to the Suez Canal. Over 5% of total world oil production transits past Yemen's coastline and passes through the "oil choke point" of Bab el-Mandab.[12] At its widest point, the 18-mile wide Bab el-Mandab is narrower than the Strait of Hormuz, and the width of its effective shipping lanes is only 4 miles wide.[13] This makes the strait especially vulnerable to interdiction from land and sea. Since 2002, when terrorists attacked the French oil tanker MV Limburg in the Bab el-Mandab and because of continual threats from pirates operating around the approaches to the Bab el-Mandab in the Gulf of Aden, an international coalition has committed significant maritime resources to ensure maritime freedom of movement off Yemen's coast.[14]

Increased instability and lack of economic opportunity could lead Yemenis, like their Somali neighbors, to resort to criminal activity offshore in Yemeni waters or piracy in international waters. Increased criminal activity could interdict the flow of energy transport or other ship borne trade in the Gulf of Aden or the Bab el-Mandab. In the short-term, shipping disruptions would negatively affect the supply of oil and other materials to Europe and the US East Coast. In the long-term, if instability continues and ships adjust routes to bypass the sea-lanes around Yemen, the entire global economy will be negatively affected. Ships sailing around the Cape of Good Hope in southern

Africa add between 8 to 15 days of travel, and increase transportation costs, as compared to using the more direct shipping routes through Yemeni waters.[15]

Besides oil and maritime influence, Yemen is also significant because of its geopolitical location. Yemen shares land borders with Saudi Arabia and Oman, two of the US's strongest allies in the Middle East. Both Saudi Arabia and Oman have consistently supported a variety of US diplomatic, military and economic policies in the region. Most notably, Oman provided bases, which the US used to launch the invasion against Al Qaeda and the Taliban in Afghanistan. Oman continues to support US regional counterterrorism efforts and has been a key partner and intermediary for ongoing Arab–Israeli peace talks.[16] Saudi Arabia has long supported US economic and energy policies, provided bases to US forces, and served as a dependable ally in the war against Al Qaeda and other terrorist organizations. Continued instability in Yemen could lead to greater internal security issues for these two allies and prevent them from greater efforts to solve regional or international issues.

Additionally, Yemen shares close geographic, economic and cultural ties with Somalia. Trade routes and smuggling routes exist between Yemen and Somalia and contribute to regional instability. Human, weapons and narcotics trafficking, and terrorist activity all move via established routes between Somalia and Yemen and onward.[17] Interdicting and eventually dismantling these networks will lead to increased regional stability and produce positive global effects. While unlikely in the near-term, it is possible that increased stability in Yemen will result in increased Somali stability that can improve the desperate situation in this failed state.

While Yemen is not a failed state like Somalia, by every measure it rapidly approaches failure. Per capita GDP, a widely recognized measure of societal prosperity, is under $1000, making Yemen the poorest nation in the Arabian Peninsula area.[18] Yemeni oil production, which constitutes the bulk of current and projected Yemeni GDP, is on the decline and future natural gas exportation will not be able to replace lost oil revenue without increases in underlying commodity prices or an increase in production and export.[19] Historically an exporter of food to other nations, Yemen's agriculture prospects are also dim. Only 3% of Yemeni land is arable, and water is equally scarce.[20] In search of greater profits, Yemeni farmers quickly deplete their ground water supply by replacing food crops with the water intensive narcotic plant Qat.[21] Recent estimates place the unemployment rate in Yemen at 35% with the illiteracy rate at over 50%.[22] Without foreign assistance, it is unlikely that any pro-democratic movement will be able to stabilize and improve the local economy. Low quality of life, lack of economic opportunity, rampant corruption and the government elites' plunder of already limited foreign aid all point toward increased social and political strife and a need for external intervention.[23]

Politically and socially, Yemen faces huge stability challenges. President Saleh had ruled Yemen for the past 30 years through an "autocratic, patronage style of governing" that pits opposition groups, tribal, military and business leaders against one another.[24] Saleh's rule led to oppression, factionalism, allowed terrorism to flourish, and inspired a variety of contra-governmental movements, ranging from secessionist, to religious to pro-democratic.[25] Outside of the major population centers in Yemen, the "well armed" tribes, led by entrenched traditional leaders are the *de facto* government.[26]

The pro-democratic youth movement that sparked the most recent protests in Yemen is not currently postured to govern in a post-Saleh country. Despite being able to build an anti-Saleh alliance among tribal leaders, dissidents, military defectors, and intellectuals, the nascent movement lacks national organization and a central leader.[27]

So, Why Yemen, And Why Now? Despite the uncertainty that President Saleh's departure generates, Yemen has the potential to shake off its violent and unproductive past. Saleh was the most significant impediment to reducing corruption, developing the economy, and significantly improving the welfare of the citizenry. The US has a fleeting window of opportunity to work with the Yemeni opposition groups, regional allies, the international community, and the Yemeni people to achieve a positive "new beginning" and stop Yemen's descent to state failure. Unfortunately, past US policy, as one Yemen expert has stated, "is adrift," and is not likely make any significant gains in Yemen.[28]

The Evolution of Current US–Yemen Policy

Because it has never been a center of US attention, one could best describe policy towards Yemen as intermittent and reactionary. US–Yemeni relations have a relatively short and contentious history, beginning with the US's recognition of the Republic of Yemen in 1962.[29] Between 1967 and 2000, all aspects of bilateral relations between the US and Yemen were suspended because of three significant foreign policy clashes. Yemen aligned itself with the Soviet Union in the Cold War, proclaimed support for Saddam Hussein during the First Gulf War, and fought a border war with longtime US ally Saudi Arabia in the 1990s.[30] However, between 1990 and 2000, to gain the international community's support, Yemen's leadership actively sought to improve relations with Saudi Arabia and the US by settling border disputes and holding presidential elections.[31] Yemeni outreach attempts were quickly marginalized as the government increasingly focused on domestic security issues. To defeat a secessionist movement in 1994, President Saleh employed thousands of ex-Soviet jihad fighters against the Marxists in South Yemen.[32] Saleh's empowerment of jihadists and his own brutal tactics of repression drew considerable international condemnation and produced significant unintended consequences that would bring US–Yemeni relations to the fore in 2000.[33]

In 1999, in an effort to improve relations with Yemen, the Clinton Administration signed a bilateral agreement to fuel US Navy vessels at the Yemeni port of Aden.[34] In 2000, Yemen-based Al Qaeda terrorists conducted a deadly attack against the USS Cole while anchored at Aden. As the Yemeni government was working with the US to investigate the bombing and pursue those responsible, additional Al Qaeda terrorists conducted the September 11, 2001 attacks in the US. With the US shift to a war footing, Yemen's foreign policy importance rose dramatically. Saleh's previous pro-jihadist stance had allowed Al Qaeda and other extremist groups to flourish in Yemen. The US identified these linkages and resultantly opened a "new front" on the global war on terror in Yemen between 2001 to 2004.[35] As such, the renewed relations and subsequent US policy focused very narrowly on security and counterterrorism.[36] Despite US displeasure with Saleh's authoritarian rule, the US worked with him and his regime because of his pledge to support US counter-terror operations and his newfound support for the US's anti-Saddam Hussein position.[37]

Ambassador Hull, also a State Department counterterrorism expert, mounted a concerted effort to overhaul US policy towards Yemen during his 2001-2004 tenure as ambassador. Sensing that Yemeni Al Qaeda operatives were a symptom of the greater political, economic and social issues, Ambassador Hull revised US-Yemeni policy to reflect his vision of Yemen as a counter terror "partner, not target" and as a country where development was likely to bring about greater stability and security.[38] As a result, the US began to resume security assistance efforts to include training and equipping Yemeni Special Operations Forces and Coast Guard to initiate small-scale development projects in some of the less stable areas in Yemen.[39]

Despite Ambassador Hull's efforts to move to a more holistic approach, policy towards Yemen neglected widespread economic development and remained focused on counterterrorism. US aid to Yemen that had increased from 2001 to 2003 dropped to a trickle, $4.6 million, in 2006 because of the perceived success of the partnered counter-terror operations.[40] Saleh and his government acted as good counterterrorism partners, and US policy, despite several diplomats' concerns with Saleh's authoritarian rule, rewarded and supported his regime.

In 2004, the Houthis, a Yemeni Shia tribe, launched a series of protests against what they called Saleh's illegitimate rule. These protests turned into a bloody five-year civil war that further destabilized Yemen, and took Yemeni security forces focus off pursuing Al Qaeda terrorists.[41] Saleh's heavy-handed tactics during the Houthi rebellion, his poor human rights record, other repressive regime actions, and most importantly, corruption kept the US from fully supporting Saleh and investing more meaningful amounts of development dollars in Yemen.[42] Despite the mounting concerns with Saleh, the US chose to continue to work with him, largely because he was the duly elected president of Yemen, rather than oppose his rule. This predisposition led to a series of confusing and seemingly contradictory US policies enacted since 2009.

Following President Barak Obama's election in 2008, the new Administration initiated a Yemen policy review. The results of this review, combined with assessments by senior US Department of State and Defense officials, resulted in a new way ahead. The new policy, formally launched in 2009, centered on a "whole of government approach" where US activities would work in concert with other "international actors."[43] The new US approach sought to continue counterterrorism activities, but to attack them by addressing the root causes of instability while also building in Saleh's regime a capacity to "exercise its authority and deliver security and service to its people."[44] To implement the new strategy, the US dramatically increased aid payments to Yemen. US Department of State development and foreign military financing aid jumped from a modest $18.2 million in 2008 to $30.3 million in 2009 and $58.4 million in 2010, with $62.8 and $120.1 million projected for expenditure in 2011 and 2112 respectively.[45] The increase in US aid, however, was not a blank check for the Saleh regime. In exchange for the aid, the US expected continued military-to-military cooperation against Al Qaeda in Yemen. Additionally, Saleh's government pledged to take strong measures to reduce corruption, improve human rights and engage in a "comprehensive and inclusive national dialogue between all opposition groups and the ruling party."[46]

The new "Whole of Government" policy, regardless of its improvement over previous policies, actually strengthened the status quo in Yemen. The new policy placed demands on Saleh's regime, but ultimately reinforced its legitimacy by channeling funds through his government. Selah was able to claim credit for external funding and strengthen his image within his patronage network and among the Yemeni people. Simultaneously, the US Department of Defense provided greater "Section 1206 Security

Assistance Funds" to the Yemeni military than the Department of State provided funds for development assistance, which further empowered the Saleh regime. In 2010 alone, the US spent $72.5 million in 1206 funds on increasing the Yemeni Special Operations and Air Forces capacity to combat terrorism.[47] While aimed at defeating AQAP, US efforts to improve the effectiveness of Yemen's counter terrorism forces strengthened the very units that in the future would ably fight, at his direction, to keep Saleh in power. In the face of growing internal opposition to Saleh's rule, the US policy of working through and with Saleh created a strong impression that the US supported Saleh, to the detriment of the Yemeni people, and that the US' clear priority was combating AQAP.

In early February 2010, inspired by the abdication of Tunisia's President Ben Ali, multiple anti-Saleh groups and pro-democracy protesters took to the streets, sparking an eleven-month series of protests to remove Saleh from power.[48] With protests and regime changes erupting across the Arab world in what is now called the "Arab Spring," the US found itself unable to articulate a clear way ahead in both the broader Arab world and in Yemen. In response to the protests, the US publically supported the "home grown" self-determination movements and urged economic and political reforms, without calling for Saleh to step down.[49]

As the protests in Yemen gained traction, the US began issuing a series of vacillating policy statements that weakened US credibility. In May 2011, US State Department officers testifying before the House of Representatives' Foreign Affairs Committee stated that the US "supports a peaceful and orderly transfer of power in accordance with the Yemeni people's demand for better governance that is more responsive to their needs and aspirations."[50] This position again stopped short of demanding a change in Yemeni leadership. Rather, administration officials called on Saleh to work with the protestors to fulfill some of their demands. As Saleh managed to counter the protestors and maintain his hold on power, the US again modified its position and lent its support for a Gulf Cooperation Council (GCC) transition plan.[51]

The transition plan proposed a political leadership shift that would "keep power in the hands of established political actors rather than letting it develop in the grass roots movement that has emerged."[52] While this slight policy shift did not completely abandon the US policy of internal Yemeni self-determination, it clearly discounted the probability of its success, and the US continued "its regular engagement with the government, including President Ali Abdullah Saleh." [53] The US stopped short of demanding that Saleh sign the agreement and again left Saleh's government to determine its course of action. This subtle shift was not lost on any of the Yemeni pro-democracy protesters who believed that the GCC agreement and US support for it "serves in the interests of the dominant powers and some of the states in the region, but it does not fit with aspirations of Yemeni youth."[54] Meanwhile the US, as part of a NATO mission, was targeting and bombing Libyan military forces in support of Libyan Opposition fighters. This fact was not lost on the anti-Saleh opposition.

Through the late summer and early winter of 2011, the US continued its "watch and wait" approach. US counter-terrorism operations continued, US aid to Yemen remained suspended and the US continued to lend its support to the GCC transition plan. Meanwhile, violence continued to rage as government forces and protestors clashed in Yemen, and the US issued additional statements condemning violence and asking Saleh to step down.[55] Finally in mid-December 2011, President Saleh, feeling the pressure of the international community, the GCC, and most significantly the Yemeni opposition parties agreed to resign and hold elections in early 2012.

While it is conceivable that a more aggressive US approach could have hastened Saleh's departure, the US's need to continue to conduct counter-terrorism operations and its long history of working with Saleh dominated the US's vacillating, wait and see approach. Now that Saleh is out of power, the US must redraft the majority of its old policies designed to support Saleh. The US must validate old interests and identify new objectives based on the multitude of emergent challenges in the region.

US Interests in the Arabian Peninsula, Yemen and Its Environs

The Arabian Peninsula, its environs and the nation of Yemen are geopolitically significant to the US. The Arabian Peninsula is host to some of the US's most loyal and supportive allies, is abundant in natural resources, sits astride several key global maritime and land trade routes, contains Islam's most holy places and has served as the ideological birthplace and operational theater for the most deadly global terrorist group, Al Qaeda. Because of the area's importance, the US has identified several vital and other lesser interests in the region that it must secure to achieve US national and international goals and objectives.

The current U.S. National Security Strategy identifies eight vital interests that form the basis for all US policy:

1. Secure the American population
2. Prevent nuclear proliferation, especially possession by violent extremists
3. Disrupt, dismantle and defeat Al Qaeda
4. Achieve peace between Israel and its neighbors

5. Rebuild our economic strength which benefits global prosperity

6. Promote universal values around the world, especially in fragile democracies

7. Shape an international order that promotes a just peace

8. Combat global climate change[56]

Of these eight interests, protecting the American people and defeating Al Qaeda are clearly interests that the US can secure in Yemen and the greater Arabian Peninsula, through the right set of policies and actions. Continued instability in Yemen could have a significant effect on global trade and the US's desire to rebuild economically and can take the region's attention and resources away from another key interest – promoting Israeli-Palestinian peace. How the US pursues its interests in Yemen, the Arabian Peninsula and other Arab Spring nations will set the tone for further advancing stability, democratic institutions and long-term peace.

The US Counterterrorism Strategy identifies several additional interests that support the National Security Strategy objectives of protecting Americans and defeating Al Qaeda and its affiliates:

1. Eliminate safe havens

2. Build enduring counterterrorism partnerships and capabilities

3. Degrade links between Al Qaeda and its affiliates and adherents

4. Counter Al Qaeda ideology and its resonance and diminish the specific drivers of violence that Al Qaeda exploits

5. Deprive terrorists their enabling means (finance and material support)[57]

Yemen is fertile ground for developing threats to US counter-terror interests. All aspects listed above apply to the current Yemen situation. The strategy also specifically highlights the fact that AQAP is the principle object of counter-terror efforts in the region.[58] Further, echoing the 2009 strategy reassessment and the 2010 National Security Strategy, the US Government identifies that to defeat AQAP, the US must also work to stabilize the country and prevent state failure.[59] Finally, the Counterterrorism Strategy also highlights the importance of the Arabian Peninsula environs, specifically East Africa. East Africa is historically, culturally, politically, and economically tied to Yemen and other nations in the Arabian Peninsula. Al Shabaab, an Al Qaeda affiliated group that is rapidly expanding its size and influence in Somalia, represents a danger to stability in Yemen, the Arabian Peninsula and global US interests.[60]

The US Central Command (USCENTCOM) is the military headquarters that is responsible for conducting military operations and security assistance activities to help achieve national security objectives in Yemen and the greater Arabian Peninsula. To meet the goals of the National Security Strategy, the USCENTCOM commander has established a supporting regional strategy aimed at achieving the following:

1. Security of U.S. citizens and the U.S. homeland

2. Regional stability

3. Promotion of effective and legitimate governance, human rights, the rule of law, and sustained economic growth and opportunity

4. Free flow of commerce and trade within the region, through strategic maritime chokepoints, and via land based trade routes to international markets[61]

These regional interests compliment the national interests and are clearly applicable to the current unstable situation in Yemen. Should Yemen deteriorate further, it is also clear to see that it will be much harder for the US to achieve its goals in the country and region.

While the US has many vital and significant interests in Yemen and the rest of the Arabian Peninsula, the US is not the only influence in the area. Future US policy must consider regional actors and other influences in order to be most effective. It is possible for the US to secure its interests unilaterally; however, it is not probable.

Regional Influences and Other Actors

Another key conclusion of the US's 2009 Yemen policy review was that the US must work with regional allies and actors to secure its national interests. In the immediate aftermath of Yemen's "Arab Spring" protests, there was no international or regional consensus on what to do in response. The US initially backed the pro-democracy protesters and called for Saleh to step down. As Yemen's pro-democracy movement's momentum stalled, the US shifted support to the Gulf Cooperation Council initiative to remove Saleh from power. Whatever the reason for the shift in strategy, the result was significant. Experts believed that the US had significant leverage over Saleh and would be able to influence his actions. However, the US failed to broker a solution while the GCC succeeded.[62] True to the policy review conclusions, the US is currently unable to shape Yemen's future unilaterally. Any future strategies must take into account the GCC and its most powerful member nation, Saudi Arabia as central to Yemeni stability.

Traditionally the GCC has focused on regional economic issues, not security and stability initiatives. According to one regional expert, the 2011 Yemeni transition plan signified a "new era of regional activism that seems to be developing in the GCC."[63] Created in 1981, primarily as an economic organization, the GCC is comprised of six Sunni Muslim monarchies: Saudi Arabia, Kuwait, Qatar, Bahrain, Oman and the United Arab Emirates.[64] The GCC is culturally, religiously and politically opposed to Iran and has maintained relations with Yemen despite Yemen's being a republic. Besides siding with Yemeni opposition parties that resulted in brokering the Saleh transition plan, the GCC also supported anti-Gaddafi forces.[65] In stark contrast, the GCC nations quickly sent military forces to suppress pro-democracy protestors in member state Bahrain. GCC actions demonstrate the organization's desire to restore regional stability and maintain the general political, social and economic status quo among the member nations. While the GCC is most likely to achieve stability in Yemen, the organization is unlikely to press for sweeping democratic or social reforms as this would contradict their own monarchial governmental systems.

Despite its lack of experience in developing and implementing external security affairs, many in the international community believe that the GCC is best suited to assist Yemen in the immediate term. In 2010, the GCC and its member nations participated in the United Kingdom-led "Friends of Yemen" initiative.[66] At this meeting, GCC nations signaled that they shared international concerns regarding Yemen's instability and the danger it poses to "containing terrorism and ensuring the security of busy shipping channels in the Gulf of Aden and the Bab al-Mandab strait.[67] To accomplish this goal, the GCC conference attendees pledged to re-validate their 2006 commitments to provide over $3.7 billion in development aid to Yemen.[68] Western nations believe that the GCC is a suitable "honest broker" to continue to work towards stabilizing Yemen because of its significant "contact and partnerships with elite players inside this [Yemeni] network."[69]

While the April 23, 2011 GCC plan was an unprecedented political action for the trade organization and is currently the best near-term vehicle to bring change to Yemen, it does not call for a radical restructuring of the Yemeni political system. The plan's first objective was to remove Saleh and quiet the opposition parties as opposed to removing his entire government and giving power to a collection of pro-democracy opposition groups. Immediately upon Saleh's departure, the plan specified that governmental authority would pass to the vice president, who is currently a member of Saleh's political party. Additionally the plan called for the new president to establish a new transitional governing body where 50% of the members are from the current government, 40% from the opposition and 10% from "other political powers."[70]

This measure gave Saleh, through his former deputies and allies, great power to shape and control the transitional government precluding significant political change. In addition to granting immunity from prosecution to Saleh and his "aides," the agreement also stipulated that Yemen must hold a constitutional convention and then have a national referendum to approve the new constitution.[71] The agreement does not specify any actions after the constitutional referendum; however, it implies that there will be a presidential election and possibly a future election for the national assembly. Every step in the GCC transition plan allows Saleh's political party to shape the process and the results, which will not satisfy the pro-democracy protestors and other opposition groups. While not in the interests of the anti-Saleh opposition, and not as radical as some nations in the international community would like, it is a measured and conservative initiative that attracted support from all members of the GCC, especially the GCC's leading nation, Saudi Arabia.

When it comes to contacts and partnerships with Yemen, no nation has greater contact, both good and bad with Yemen than Saudi Arabia. While the GCC is leading

19

the Yemen transition of power effort, Saudi Arabia is the dominant force in the GCC and exercises the most influence and leverage over Yemen. Any future US-Yemeni policy must understand and complement, where possible, the complex history, current issues and interests of Saudi Arabia.

Saudi Arabia is the most significant outside influence in all aspects of Yemeni life. While on his deathbed, King Abdul Aziz, the founder of the modern Saudi monarchy, allegedly told his sons and grandsons to "keep Yemen weak."[72] Regardless of the truth of this statement, successive Saudi rulers have put it into practice principally by "subsidizing factional divisions ... which prevent any single group – government, tribe or military – from achieving outright superiority" in Yemeni politics.[73] To this end, Saudi Arabia has made annual payments, which experts have estimated to run as high as several billion dollars, to Yemeni leaders with little to show in return.[74] Despite the failure of past efforts to cultivate subservient Yemeni strongmen, all indications are that the Saudis are already trying to advance friendly candidates to fill the leadership vacuum that will occur after Saleh's departure.[75] In fact, Saudi Arabia's legacy patronage system and extra-governmental payments have prevented Yemen from developing key national institutions such as a functioning legislature and a corruption free executive branch that must be present to stabilize the nation.

While deeply connected with Yemen, Saudi Arabia has also clashed with Yemen in the past. Saudi Arabia intervened militarily in Yemen during the 1962 Yemeni Republican revolution and again in 2009 during a clash with Yemeni Shia Houthi rebels.[76] When Yemen sided with Saddam Hussein during the first Gulf War, Saudi Arabia, as well as other gulf nations, expelled over 800,000 Yemeni workers creating long lasting economic and social issues upon their return to Yemen.[77] Because of these actions and continual interference in Yemeni internal affairs, the Yemeni population has mixed feelings about the Saudis though recent polling indicates that 36% of the population believes that the Saudis are one of the best outside entities to help bring stability to Yemen.[78]

Despite past attempts to keep Yemen weak, or at least neutralized, current instability, and the growth and aggressiveness of AQAP has forced Saudi Arabia to reexamine its regional interests and policies towards Yemen. Saudi Arabia's vital interests are to maintain the monarchy's hold on power inside the country and to maintain its status as a hegemon in the Arabian Peninsula.[79] To achieve their vital interests, the Saudis promote regional stability, especially with their neighbors, economic expansion to placate their domestic population, and oppose destabilizing forces such as Iran and Al Qaeda. Instability in Yemen has caused the Saudis, who fear "spill-over effects," to reconsider the importance of their southern neighbor.[80] More so than potential refugee problems and the disruption of regional trade, the Saudis are now most concerned with security issues – the Houthis and AQAP. While Yemen watchers dispute the claim, the Saudis firmly believe that the northern Shia Houthi rebels are being influenced and supplied by Iran and could possibly partner with Al Qaeda to achieve greater effects against the Saudi regime.[81] Saudi Arabia has always opposed Al Qaeda and other extremist groups that sought sanctuary inside its borders. However, AQAP is the first group to specifically declare war on the Saudi regime and initiate suicide assassination attacks against members of the Saudi royal family.[82] Continued instability seriously concerns the Saudi government and has led it to look for new avenues, such as the GCC's transition initiative, to achieve its national goals. Because a Yemeni descent to state failure frightens Saudi Arabia, it will continue to work with other nations, or if necessary will work unilaterally to ensure any post-Saleh Yemen supports their interests.

Beside the GCC and Saudi Arabia, several other organizations and nations will play a key role in shaping Yemen's future. Among the twenty international members of the 2010 Friends of Yemen initiative are the United Kingdom, creator of the initiative; Germany; and the United Arab Emirates, chairing a working group on economic and governance issues; and the Netherlands with Jordan, chairing a working group on justice and rule of law issues.[83] The Friends of Yemen, including Saleh's government of Yemen representatives, developed a sweeping five-year political, economic, development and security reform plan that was to begin in 2012.[84] However, due to continued instability in Yemen, the GCC nations cancelled follow-up meetings, and the plan is currently on hold. The terms of the Friends of Yemen agreement, and the participation of leading western, gulf nations and other international institutions such as the World Trade Organization, the World Bank and the International Monetary Fund, will be key to help enact new policies in Yemen. While not a prominent participant in the Friends of Yemen initiative, the United Nations has, and will continue to play a key role in focusing international attention on Yemen. Future policies and programs, implemented by the UN, the Friends of Yemen and other international organizations and Non-governmental organizations have the potential to change the status quo in Yemen.

Often overlooked, another vitally important force that affects Yemen's future, lies across the Gulf of Aden in Somalia. Somalia and Yemen are historically and economically linked, though not necessarily in productive or constructive ways. During the Yemeni civil wars, Yemenis fled the violence to Somalia; when Somalia descended into chaos in the 1990s, Somalis received automatic asylum in Yemen.[85] Because of this migration, businesses and criminals developed licit- and illicit-trade and smuggling routes between the Horn of Africa and the Arabian Peninsula. Current UN estimates indicate that the majority of weapons that insurgents and warlords use in Somalia come from Yemen and move via these smuggling networks alongside other illegal cargoes.[86] Additionally, Al Qaeda has learned to exploit these smuggling networks to move money, arms, leadership, and foot soldiers throughout the region.[87] Currently, it does not appear that Al Shababb, the Somalia based Al Qaeda group, is synchronizing operations with AQAP. However, Al Shababb has announced support for AQAP, and the continued instability in Yemen is likely to bring these two very dangerous factions together.[88] It is possible that, given an effective US policy in Yemen, the converse may also be true; that stability in Yemen could lead to greater stability and suppression of Al Qaeda forces in East Africa.

"New Beginning" Policy Recommendations

There is no "silver bullet," quick-fix plan to stabilize Yemen. However, the US can take advantage of the rapidly changing political landscape to create and implement a bold new strategy to shape Yemen's future. Past policies and careful study reveal several approaches and policy options that are more likely to secure vital US interests and accomplish policy objectives. The following paragraphs present some of the most salient approaches and policy options; although, recent history advises policy makers to proceed with caution. The recommendations are not all-inclusive and will not address every one of the numerous political, economic, military and social problems which plague Yemen, but serve as a good starting point to create sound policy.

While the US has always considered Yemen as an important nation in the Middle East, it has never been a US foreign policy priority. US policy makers must acknowledge that Yemeni stability is essential to achieve long-term stability in the region and accept that Yemen is now a US priority. Because of the number and breadth of challenges facing the country, the US must also approach Yemen as an enduring priority and apply a greater amount of resources towards achieving policy goals. As a priority, the US must ensure that sufficient diplomatic, economic and security assistance resources are available and are applied in a unified and consistent manner over, what will realistically be, the next few decades. Though seemingly expensive now, the costs of inaction are far greater in the future.

AQAP poses a significant threat to Yemeni internal security and US interests. Therefore, the US must continue to actively pursue and destroy key AQAP terrorists as the US establishes its new strategy and policies and works to implement them. AQAP is under stress after the killing of Al Awalki and several other high profile terrorist operatives. However, AQAP's leadership, Emir Nasir al-Wuhayshi and Deputy Zaid al-Samari, remain intact.[89] In partnership with Yemen's elite special operations forces, US Counterterrorism (CT) forces must continue to pressure AQAP leadership and key operational planners in order to spoil potential attacks against the US homeland or interests abroad. Meanwhile, CT forces must also demonstrate restraint.

Polling and expert analysis indicates most Yemenis do not approve of AQAP, AQAP leaders, and senior Al Qaeda leaders but have reservations about US and other western nations' intentions.[90] AQAP is very unpopular or somewhat unpopular with 86% of Yemenis and Bin Laden drew an even higher unpopular rating of 91%.[91] Likely because of past association with Saleh to facilitate aggressive counter terrorism efforts, 96% of Yemenis oppose current US–Yemeni security assistance cooperation.[92] Due to the tremendous negative perception of US CT operations and military assistance, US officials must limit any kinetic strikes to only the most critical targets until stability activities begin and Yemeni perceptions change. The US also needs to develop more covert and indirect methods for achieving long-term CT objectives. As a new political order forms in Yemen, it is imperative that CT operations do not undercut the new government but lead to a more positive security relationship with the Yemeni government which the population supports.

Now that the US has chosen to support the GCC plan to the detriment of the Yemeni opposition parties, especially the pro-democracy youth movement, the US needs to stay the course in the near-term. It will likely be more harmful for the US to flip-flop again, change support priorities or favor some other transition process. As much as the Yemeni people need this consistency, so too do the nations of the GCC so they can move ahead with the agreement. Beyond moral and diplomatic support, the US should work with the GCC nations to provide other critical support through them since the perception of the US in Yemen is presently poor. This may mean that the US compensates GCC nations for monies spent on development projects or provides military equipment or backfills national security forces to allow GCC observers or trainers to take an on ground role in Yemen. Additionally, the US could strengthen the capacity of the GCC by providing a staff of development experts to quicken development efforts.

Supporting the GCC to stabilize Yemen does not, however mean that the US should adopt a passive approach. The US must shape the agenda in Yemen, synchronize the long-term plans and posture for a more "hands-on" presence in Yemen when conditions permit. The US should take the lead to strengthen the Friends of Yemen organization and make it the long-term steering body for future international engagement in Yemen. The US and Friends of Yemen should work the "external" issues and long-range planning while the GCC, especially our close allies the Saudis, can work the "internal" plans and local policy implementation. Thirty-six percent of the Yemeni population see the Saudis, not the US, as the group of choice to help stabilize the country.[93] Yemenis see the Arab League, whose members include all the GCC countries in an even better light; 52% see the League as the group of choice to stabilize Yemen.[94] To increase the capability of the US to monitor and shape the GCC's nascent foreign policy and development initiatives, the US should create a formal diplomatic mission to the GCC and appoint and envoy or ambassador with a robust staff.

As conditions and perceptions of the US change in Yemen, the Friends of Yemen group can take a greater "inside" role in the country. The GCC, while a welcome and necessary group, is unlikely to take measures beyond the minimums to reestablish the status quo. The GCC has afforded Yemen special status because of its geographic location but as former Ambassador Hull stated, the GCC is "a club for rich monarchies and Yemen is neither rich nor a monarchy."[95] No GCC monarchy, as evidenced by the GCC's intervention to crush street protests in Bahrain during its initial Arab Spring protests, is interested in building a functional, effective democratic republic in Yemen. To meet the US's long-term ideological goal of promoting the creation of democratic institutions, and the stated objective to strengthen fragile democratic governments, the US must be prepared to take a more prominent role in Yemen's political evolution should the GCC's initiatives stop short of building a functioning representative government in Yemen.

Further, the US must fully support the Friends of Yemen program and significantly increase its foreign aid to Yemen. As a significant donor, the US garners greater influence in the geopolitical environment and can target funds to build the right institutions and projects to achieve long-term objectives. The billions that the Saudis give annually and the several billions that the GCC nations pledged for the Friends of Yemen program dwarf the $150 million in foreign aid that the US government budgeted to support Yemen for 2012.[96] US contributions need not compete with the GCC; rather they should be complementary. The US Department of State has a well thought-out development plan, the USAID 2010-2012 Yemen Country Strategy, that it can adjust, reinvigorate and even expand now that Saleh has stepped aside.[97] USAID has the development experience, staff and capacity to assist the GCC nations, who lack these critical capabilities, to implement their funded projects in Yemen.[98] While it will be unpopular to increase foreign aid to Yemen in an era of budget cutbacks, a modest investment in Yemen now will preclude greater costs in the future as instability and economic ruin broaden. In a nation that has a $5 billion annual gross domestic product, significant US aid contribution increases can have tremendous impact.[99] Any pre-conflict stabilization costs, especially when viewed in conjunction with Friends of Yemen aid,

IMF and World Bank programs, would be a fraction of the cost associated with deploying US troops to a failing state to conduct foreign internal defense or counter insurgency operations. Additionally, the US can use its influence in the United Nations to raise the awareness and importance of the Yemeni situation to the entire international community.

Finally, the US must carefully continue security force assistance operations to prevent further instability and continue counter terrorism operations. The majority of US–Yemeni military-to-military contact, and security assistance funding, since 2001 has focused on Yemen's special operations forces who are responsible for conducting counter terror operations.[100] Unfortunately, Saleh's son Ahmed commands the Yemeni SOF and recent reporting states he is currently leading operations against opposition and pro-democracy protestors.[101] The US must leverage its positive relationship with Yemeni forces to ensure that they provide stability and defer to transitional government and later permanent civilian government control. Focus on this task may prevent the US from aggressively pursuing AQAP, but in the end, it is the most important task.

Currently, one-half of the Yemeni Army has defected to the opposition under the leadership of its commander Ali Muhsin al-Ahmar.[102] While it is unknown what will happen to the Yemeni armed forces after the transition agreement, the US must focus its efforts on limiting any further fracturing and factionalization of the military. Finally, Yemen's military currently employs over 600,000 people who, according to experts, provide income for family members constituting one quarter of the Yemeni population.[103] Should the Yemeni military disintegrate, the social and economic impact would be crippling given the current 35% unemployment rate.[104] The Yemeni military can be the nation's greatest source of stability or instability in this critical time, and US policy must carefully achieve the former.

Risks

While it is clear that the US must implement a new US-Yemeni policy, doing so is not a risk free endeavor. Policy makers must understand that, despite the best intentions and a carefully crafted strategy, failure may occur for two primary reasons, changing priorities and Yemeni dissatisfaction with the nature and pace of change.

The challenges that face Yemen are broad-based and the obstacles to stability are deeply entrenched in every facet of society. Solutions will likely take decades, not years, to succeed. This requires that not only the US, but also key members of the international community such as the GCC, continue to make Yemen a priority. Solutions require building new institutions such as a functional legislature and initiating investment and development efforts to promote economic growth and diversification. Efforts such as these require a long-term commitment of resources, both human and financial, and in the case of the US, will likely span multiple budgeting cycles and presidential administrations. Should the US adjust its priorities to focus on a new global "hot-spot" such as China, Iran, or Sub-Saharan Africa, Yemen is not likely to stabilize or reform itself. If the GCC discontinues its aggressive foreign policy campaign, fails to provide critical development and economic funding or if its member nations become embroiled in domestic stability or other security challenges, Yemen's path to stability and prosperity will abruptly end. The US must play a critical role to keep Yemen in the forefront as an international and regional priority in order to secure national interests.

Any progress towards Yemeni stability can also fail from within. After decades of internal conflict, repression, and poverty, the Yemeni people have spoken, demanding change. They expect that the GCC and the US will deliver results. Should conditions not improve in Yemen as fast as the people expect, they will likely withdraw their support for the GCC plan and seek alternate ways to affect change. Because a diverse citizenry will measure satisfaction in a variety of ways, implementation of initiatives, programs, and reforms must be equally broad and well conceived. In this light, asymmetry of progress is a very real risk to success.[105] Should the Yemeni economy not improve, the people may rise up again to demand that Saleh's replacement or even the new legislature step aside, even if the government has been successfully reforming. Should the military remain under the control of Saleh's family and no counterbalancing governmental or social institutions develop, all progress and reform could easily stall. Finally, should the new government's policies only benefit the country's elites, then the people are very likely to take to the streets again. While this is not an exhaustive list of scenarios, it is easy to see how difficult it will be to balance the delivery of effects to the Yemeni people to galvanize their support for their government. Should stabilization and reform falter for any reason, violent actors such as AQAP will undoubtedly exploit the people's dissatisfaction and stability in the greater Arabian Peninsula will suffer.

Conclusion

The situation in Yemen continues to evolve, but does not improve. President Saleh has left power; however, he and his family have not permanently left Yemen. Uninfluenced and undeterred, Saleh will continue to arrest Yemen's much needed political and economic transformation. Inaction, or poor action at this opportune time, will make it difficult for the US to secure its national and regional interests. The US must take advantage of President Saleh's departure to usher in an era of change in Yemen.

The US must acknowledge that stability in the greater Arabian Peninsula is dependent on stability in Yemen. Social strife, a deteriorating economy, dwindling natural resources and political and ethnic conflict all undermine stability. Most important to the US, AQAP remains a credible and capable group that intensifies Yemeni instability and threatens the US homeland. Because of the complexity and depth of Yemeni problems, successful military operations will not unilaterally defeat AQAP or secure the numerous national policy objectives in the region. Success requires that the US, as the leader of an international effort, makes solving Yemen's complex set of problems a foreign policy priority.

Correspondingly, the US must apply sufficient military, economic, development, and diplomatic resources to arrest Yemen's descent to failure. Already committed to support the GCC transition plan, the US should craft and commit to a long-term policy to stabilize Yemen as a leading Friends of Yemen nation. Development and careful support to pro-democracy and reform elements will assist the US in reestablishing a positive and constructive image in Yemen and the region. At the current time, the only way the US can achieve immediate positive effects in Yemen is to work closely with influential regional powers and the international community.

Now more than ever, the US must clearly take action to support change and bring about the better future that Yemeni's desire. US national security depends on nothing less than preventing the next Afghanistan from occurring in Yemen. To do this, the US must act consistently and enact a comprehensive, enduring policy to stabilize Yemen.

Endnotes

[1] David Batty, "Yemen violence leaves scores dead," September 24, 2011, http://www.guardian.co.uk/world/2011/sep/24/yemen-clashes-leave-16-dead (accessed February 5, 2012).

[2] Ibid.

[3] Barak H. Obama, *Statement by President Obama on the Signing of the GCC-Brokered Agreement in Yemen* (Washington, DC: The Whitehouse, November 23, 2012) http://www.whitehouse.gov/the-press-office/2011/11/23/statement-president-obama-signing-gcc-brokered-agreement-yemen (accessed February 5, 2012).

[4] Sam Stein, "Lieberman: The United States Must Pre-Emptively Act In Yemen," March 18, 2010, http://www.huffingtonpost.com/2009/12/27/lieberman-the-united-stat_n_404241 (accessed February 5, 2012).

[5] Edmund J. Hull, High-Value Target (Washington, DC: Potomac Books, 2011), xxix.

[6] Aaron Karp, "Chapter 2. Completing the Count, Civilian Firearms," in *Small Arms Survey 2007: Guns and the City,* ed. Eric G Berman, Kieth Krause, Emile LeBrun, and Glenn McDonald (New York, NY: Cambridge University Press) http://www.smallarmssurvey.org/fileadmin/docs/A-Yearbook/2007/en/full/Small-Arms-Survey-2007-Chapter-02-EN.pdf (accessed February 12, 2010) 46-48.

[7] Ginny Hill and Gerd Nonneman, "Yemen, Saudi Arabia and the Gulf States: Elite Politics, Street Protests and Regional Diplomacy," May 2011, http://www.chathamhouse.org/sites/default/files/19237_0511yemen_gulfbp.pdf (accessed February 5, 2012) 15.

[8] Alistair Harris, "Exploiting Grievances: Al-Qaeda in the Arabian Peninsula," in *Yemen on the Brink*, ed. Christopher Boucek and Marina Ottaway (Washington, D.C: Carnegie Endowment for International Peace, 2010), 35.

[9] James Phillips, "Yemen: US Policy Implications of President Saleh's Resignation Offer," April 25, 2011, http://www.heritage.org/research/reports/2011/04/yemen-us-policy-implications-of-president-salehs-resignation-offer (accessed February 5, 2012).

[10] Christopher Boucek, "Yemen After Saleh's Return and Awlaki's Exit," October 27, 2011, http://www.carnegieendowment.org/2011/10/27/yemen-after-saleh-s-return-and-awlaki-s-exit/8kpb (accessed Feburary 7, 2012).

[11] Energy Information Administration, "Country Analysis Briefs: Yemen," February 2011, http://www.eia.gov/countries/cab.cfm?fips=YM (accessed on February 5, 2012).

[12] Energy Information Administration, "Country Analysis Briefs: World Oil Transit Chokepoints," February 2011, http://www.eia.gov/cabs/world_oil_transit_chokepoints/Full.html (accessed on November 14, 2011).

[13] Ibid.

[14]Ibid.

[15]Ibid.

[16]Kenneth Katzman, Oman: Reform, Security, and U.S. Policy (Washington, DC: Library of Congress, Congressional Research Service, August 26, 2011), summary.

[17]Ginny Hill and Sally Healy, "Yemen and Somalia: Terrorism, Shadow Networks and the Limitations of State Building Transcript," interview by Jeremy Bowen, BBC, October 20, 2010, http://www.chathamhouse.org/sites/default/files/public/Meetings/Meeting%20Transcripts/201010 yemensomalia.pdf (accessed on February 5, 2012), 8-10.

[18]Hill and Nonneman, "Yemen, Saudi Arabia and the Gulf States: Elite Politics, Street Protests and Regional Diplomacy," 3.

[19]The World Bank Group, Sana'a Office. Yemen Quarterly Economic Review, Autumn/Winter 2010, 1-3. Some Yemen experts, such as Gregory Johansen and Bernard Haykel, state that Yemen is on the verge of running out of oil in the next few years and will be unable to replace this revenue. Based on the author's basic calculations based on current production figures, and barring new discoveries, Yemen will continue to produce oil for up to 28 years and can produce natural gas for 944 years. Because of instability, oil companies have not fully explored Yemen's concessions and have not attempted to use advanced oil recovery technologies. Both of these measures could lead to an increase in Yemeni proved and probable reserves. Yemen is not in danger of immediately running out of oil as some alarmist experts say, however their point is still valid; Yemen must diversify their economy or face ruin when the oil does run out.

[20]CIA World Fact Book, "Middle East: Yemen," November 8, 2011, https://www.cia.gov/library/publications/the-world-factbook/geos/ym.html (accessed on November 14, 2011).

[21]The World Bank Group, Yemen Quarterly Economic Review, 10-11.

[22]Christopher Boucek, "Yemen: Avoiding a Downward Spiral," in Yemen on the Brink, ed. Christopher Boucek and Marina Ottaway (Washington, D.C: Carnegie Endowment for International Peace, 2010), 2.

[23]Ibid., 9.

[24]Gregory D. Johnsen, "Policy Innovation Memorandum No. 8," (New York: Council on Foreign Relations Press, September 2011), 2.

[25]Gregory D. Johnsen, "Well Gone Dry," The American Interest, November/December 2006, http://www.the-american-interest.com/article.cfm?piece=195 (accessed on November 14, 2011).

[26]Hull, High-Value Target, xxvii.

[27]Kristin Smith Diwan, "Un-unified Oppositions in Bahrain and Yemen," interview by Bernard Gwertzman, Council on Foreign Relations, March 23, 2011, http://www.cfr.org/middle-east/un-unified-oppositions-bahrain-yemen/p24464 (accessed on February 5, 2012).

[28]Johnsen, "Policy Innovation Memorandum No. 8," 1.

[29]US Department of State, Background Note: Yemen, January 18, 2012, http://www.state.gov/r/pa/ei/bgn/35836.htm (accessed on February 5, 2012).

[30]Ibid.

[31]Ibid.

[32]Johnsen, "Well Gone Dry."

[33]Ibid.

[34]Jeremy M. Sharp, *Yemen: Background and U.S. Relations* (Washington, DC: Library of Congress, Congressional Research Service, October 6, 2011), 10.

[35]Ibid.

[36]Boucek, "Yemen: Avoiding a Downward Spiral," 24.

[37]Hull, *High-Value Target*,10-11,58.

[38]Ibid.,18-26.

[39]Ibid., 46-47.

[40]Gregory Johnsen, "Yemen Tensions at the Tipping Point," interview by Bernard Gwertzman, Council on Foreign Relations, June 2, 2011, http://www.cfr.org/yemen/yemen-tensions-tipping-point/p25177 (accessed on February 5, 2012).

[41]Christopher Boucek, "War in Saada: From Local Insurrection to National Challenge," in *Yemen on the Brink*, ed. Christopher Boucek and Marina Ottaway (Washington, D.C: Carnegie Endowment for International Peace, 2010), 57-59.

[42]Sharp, *Yemen: Background and U.S. Relations*, 10-11.

[43]Daniel Benjamin, "U.S. Counter Terrorism Strategy in Yemen," September 8, 2010, http://www.state.gov/j/ct/rls/rm/2010/147296 (accessed on February 5, 2012).

[44]Ibid.

[45]Sharp, *Yemen: Background and U.S. Relations*, 12.

[46]Benjamin, "U.S. Counter Terrorism Strategy in Yemen."

[47]Nina M. Serafino, *Security Assistance Reform: "Section 1206" Background and Issues for Congress,* (Washington, DC: Library of Congress, Congressional Research Service, January 13, 2012), 26.

[48]Jane Novak, "In Yemen, Many Protests, One Villain," February 12, 2011, http://atlanticsentinel.com/2011/02/in-yemen-many-protests-one-villain (accessed February 5, 2012).

[49]Michael H. Posner and Tamara C. Wittes, "Shifting Sands: Political Transitions in the Middle East, Part 2," May 5, 2011, http://www.state.gov/j/drl/rls/rm/2011/162755 (accessed February 5, 2012).

[50]Ibid.

[51]Janet Sanderson, "U.S. Policy in Yemen," July, 19,2011, http://www.state.gov/p/nea/rls/rm/168850.htm (accessed February 6, 2012).

[52]Hill and Nonneman, "Yemen, Saudi Arabia and the Gulf States: Elite Politics, Street Protests and Regional Diplomacy," 3.

[53]Sanderson, "U.S. Policy in Yemen."

[54]Louis Charbonneau, "U.N. Council condemns Yemen violence urges deal," October 22,2011, http://thestar.com.my/news/story.asp?file=/2011/10/22/worldupdates/2011-10-22T025316Z_01_NOOTR_RTRMDNC_0_-600564-1&sec=Worldupdates (accessed February 6, 2012).

[55]Victoria Newland, "Violence in Yemen," November 12, 2011, http://www.state.gov/r/pa/prs/ps/2011/11/177041.htm (accessed February 6, 2012).

[56]Barak H. Obama, *National Security Strategy, May 2010* (Washington, DC: The White House, May 2010), 4-5.

[57]Barak H. Obama, *National Strategy for Counterterrorism, June 2011* (Washington, DC: The White House, June 2011), 8-10.

[58]Ibid.,14.

[59]Ibid.

[60]Ibid., 14-15.

[61]James N. Mattis, *United States Central Command, Commander's Posture Statement*, Posture Statement presented before the Senate Armed Services Committee, March 1, 2011, http://www.centcom.mil/en/about-centcom/posture-statement (accessed February 6, 2012).

[62]Johnsen, "Yemen Tensions at the Tipping Point."

[63]Thomas W. Lippman, "Yemen Crisis Spurs Regional Activism," April 25, 2011, http://www.cfr.org/yemen/yemen-crisis-spurs-regional-activism/p24766 (accessed February 6, 2012).

[64]Ibid.

[65]Hill and Nonneman, "Yemen, Saudi Arabia and the Gulf States: Elite Politics, Street Protests and Regional Diplomacy," 3.

[66]Ibid., 4.

[67]Ibid.

[68]Ibid., 13-14.

[69]Ibid., 5.

[70]Yemen Post Staff, "GCC Proposal to solve the Yemen Crisis," April 24, 2011, http://www.yemenpost.net/Detail123456789.aspx?ID=3&SubID=3482 (accessed February 6, 2012).

[71]Ibid.

[72]Ellen Knickmeyer, "Trouble Down South," July 5, 2012, http://www.foreignpolicy.com/articles/2011/07/05/trouble_down_south?page=full (accessed February 6, 2012).

[73]Johnsen, "Well Gone Dry."

[74]Knickmeyer, "Trouble Down South."

[75]Bernard Haykel, "Yemen's Uncertain Political Future," interview by Bernard Gwertzman, Council on Foreign Relations, June 7, 2011, http://www.cfr.org/yemen/yemens-uncertain-political-future/p25205 (accessed on February 5, 2012).

[76]Knickmeyer, "Trouble Down South."

[77]Sharp, *Yemen: Background and U.S. Relations*, 7.

[78]Glevum Associates, "2011 Yemen Stability Survey," March, 2011, http://glevumassociates.com/doc/survey_YemenStability-2011.pdf (accessed February 6, 2012), 20.

[79]Nima Khorrami Assl, "Saudi Arabia's counter-revolutionary regional policy: The case of Yemen," October 13, 2011, http://www.defenceviewpoints.co.uk/articles-and-analysis/saudi-arabias-counter-revolutionary-regional-policy-the-case-of-yemen (accessed February 7, 2012).

[80]Ibid.

[81]Zuhair al-Harithi, "Understanding Yemen's Troubles: A Saudi Perspective," http://www.arabinsight.org/aiarticles/228.pdf (accessed February 7, 2012) 80-85.

[82]John Rollins, *Al Qaeda and Affiliates: Historical Perspective, Global Presence, and Implications for U.S. Policy* (Washington, DC: Library of Congress, Congressional Research Service, January 25, 2011) 17-18.

[83]Marina Ottaway and Christopher Boucek, "Stabilizing a Failing State," in *Yemen on the Brink*, ed. Christopher Boucek and Marina Ottaway (Washington, D.C: Carnegie Endowment for International Peace, 2010), 96-98.

[84]"Author Not Provided," "Friends of Yemen Chairmen's Statement," September 24, 2010, http://centralcontent.fco.gov.uk/resources/en/pdf/central-content-pdfs/middle-east/friends-of-yemen-statement (accessed February 7, 2012).

[85]Hill and Healy, "Yemen and Somalia: Terrorism, Shadow Networks and the Limitations of State Building,"9.

[86]Ibid., 9-10.

[87]Ibid., 8-9.

[88]Ibid., 4-9.

[89]Ibid., 8.

[90]Ottaway and Boucek, "Stabilizing a Failing State," 91-92.

[91]Glevum Associates, "2011 Yemen Stability Survey,"19.

[92]Ibid., 26-29.

[93]Ibid.,16.

[94]Ibid.

[95]Hull, *High-Value Target*, 122.

[96]Ottaway and Boucek, "Stabilizing a Failing State," 98-99.

[97]USAID, "2010-2012 Yemen Country Strategy," February 11, 2010, http://www.usaid.gov/locations/middle_east/documents/yemen/USAIDYemen2010-2012Strategy.pdf (accessed February 7, 2012) 1-13.

[98]Ottaway and Boucek, "Stabilizing a Failing State,"91-97.

[99]Sharp, *Yemen: Background and U.S. Relations,* 10-11.

[100]Hill and Nonneman, "Yemen, Saudi Arabia and the Gulf States: Elite Politics, Street Protests and Regional Diplomacy," 16.

[101]Boucek, "Yemen After Saleh's Return and Awlaki's Exit."

[102]Johnsen, "Policy Innovation Memorandum No. 8," 1.

[103]Novak, "One Yemen, Many Protests, One Villian."

[104]Boucek, "Yemen: Avoiding a Downward Spiral," 2.

[105]COL Scott McConnell proposed that the primary risk associated with implementing a multi-faceted policy was that of asymmetric policy implementation. Success or failure of the policy is not only determined by the policy actions but also by the proportional delivery of effects to the population in the political, economic, social, security and governmental areas. Scott McConnell, Project Advisor U.S. Army War College, discussion with author, February 24, 2012.

www.ingramcontent.com/pod-product-compliance
Lightning Source LLC
Chambersburg PA
CBHW081802280526
45789CB00008B/2970